First World War
and Army of Occupation
War Diary
France, Belgium and Germany

20 DIVISION
Divisional Troops
Machine Gun Corps
20 Battalion
15 March 1918 - 28 February 1919

WO95/2108/3

The Naval & Military Press Ltd
www.nmarchive.com
Published in association with The National Archives

Published by

The Naval & Military Press Ltd

Unit 10 Ridgewood Industrial Park,

Uckfield, East Sussex,

TN22 5QE England

Tel: +44 (0) 1825 749494

www.naval-military-press.com

www.nmarchive.com

This diary has been reprinted in facsimile from the original. Any imperfections are inevitably reproduced and the quality may fall short of modern type and cartographic standards.

© **Crown Copyright**
Images reproduced by permission of The National Archives, London, England, 2015.

Contents

Document type	Place/Title	Date From	Date To
Miscellaneous	2108/3		
Miscellaneous	20 Div 20 Bn Machine Gun Corps 1918 Mar-1919 Feb		
Miscellaneous	History of The 20th Battalion Machine Gun Corps.		
Heading	20th Divisional M.Gs. Battalion Formed 15.3.18 From 59th-60th-61st And 217th M.G. Cos.		
War Diary	Libermont	15/03/1918	31/03/1918
War Diary	Farm House (Sheet 62 D) T20 a 80.10.	01/04/1918	07/04/1918
War Diary	Sheet Dieppe 16	08/04/1918	11/04/1918
War Diary	Sheet Abbeville 14	12/04/1918	19/04/1918
War Diary	Sheet Lens II	20/04/1918	30/04/1918
War Diary	Cambligneul (Sheet Len II)	01/05/1918	02/05/1918
War Diary	Marqueffles Farm (Sheet Lens II)	03/05/1918	09/05/1918
War Diary	Scotts Camp Carency	10/05/1918	30/05/1918
War Diary	Scotts Camp Carency Sheet X16 d.4.4	01/06/1918	30/06/1918
War Diary	Scotts Camp Carency (X16.d.4.4 Sheet 44 B)	01/07/1918	24/08/1918
Heading	20th Battn. M.G.C. No. M.G. 2/923. Herewith War Diary for September, 1918.		
War Diary	Scott Camp Carency	27/08/1918	30/08/1918
War Diary	Scotts Camp Carency X 16 d.4.4 Sheet 44 B	01/09/1918	25/09/1918
War Diary	Ref Sheet 44a S W 1/20,000 Barrage Position T 22 c 7520 & T28c 75 50 Advanced Qroup Hqrs T 28 b 35 80 2 Guns On Hank T17 d 30 50 Objective Triumpnova Scotta, Britannia & Brandy Trenches Or T24 & 30 of Fresnoy.	27/09/1918	28/09/1918
War Diary	Scotts Camp Carency X16 d 40.40	28/09/1918	29/09/1918
War Diary	Scotts Camp Carency Sheet 44B X.16 d 4. 4	01/10/1918	03/10/1918
War Diary	(Sheet 44A)	03/10/1918	07/10/1918
War Diary	Sheet 44 B	07/10/1918	14/10/1918
War Diary	La Taieuloye Sheet 44B	14/10/1918	31/10/1918
War Diary	Cambrai (Valenciennes Sheet)	01/11/1918	03/11/1918
War Diary	Rieux	04/11/1918	04/11/1918
War Diary	Sommaing	07/11/1918	07/11/1918
War Diary	Mareshes	08/11/1918	08/11/1918
War Diary	St. Waast	09/11/1918	09/11/1918
War Diary	Feignies	10/11/1918	23/11/1918
War Diary	La Pissotiau	24/11/1918	24/11/1918
War Diary	Sepmeries	25/11/1918	25/11/1918
War Diary	Avesnes-Les Aubert	26/11/1918	27/11/1918
War Diary	Cambrai	28/11/1918	30/11/1918
War Diary	Marieux (Lens 11 Sheet)	01/12/1918	31/12/1918
Heading	H.Q. 20th Division I forwards herewith my War Diary for January, 1918		
War Diary	Marieux (Lens 11 Sheet)	21/01/1919	21/01/1919
War Diary	Marieux (Lens 11 Sheet)	05/01/1919	27/01/1919
Heading	20th Batt. Machine Gun Corps. 20th Division "A" Herewith copy of War Diary for February 1919		
War Diary	Marieux Lens II Sheet	02/02/1919	28/02/1919

21/08/13

20 DIV.

20. BN MACHINE GUN CORPS

1918 MAR — 1919 FEB

HISTORY OF THE 20TH BATTALION MACHINE GUN CORPS.

In December, 1915, 4 Machine Gun Companies were formed at Belton Park, Grantham. 3 of these Coys. embarked from Southampton for Le Havre on the 22-3-16; owing to the presence of submarines only one boat got across, the remainder made many attempts but did not reach Le Havre till 8 days later. Each Company was attached to one of the following Brigades - 59, 60, 61, and since the Battalion was formed they have been known as A, B, & C Coys, respectively. They were in Command of Major Birch, Major Godson, and Captain Glascott.
The 4th Company was 217, commanded by Captain Stevens who brought it out to this Division on 24-3-17 and it is now known as "D" Coy. The Companies were with the Division on the Canal Bank, near Ypres, until they all went out for a rest early in May, to Calais for a few days, where the troops enjoyed the fine weather with plenty of sea bathing and all kinds of sport. In July during a hostile attack "B" and "C" Coys. were called upon to assist the Australians and Canadians near Fleurbaix. This was the first time they had experienced gas.

Guillemont. During this battle the Companies suffered severe casualties and won many decorations, Captain Glascott was sent down with Shell-shock, Major Godson, although badly wounded in the head remained with his Company until March 1917, when he returned home owing to his age. All were personally congratuated by their Corps Commander, the Earl of Cavan. A few days afterwards they were again fighting hard at Les Boeufs, Morval, and Guideclurt.
From the 11-10-16 to 29-11-16 the time was spent in resting and reconstructing Units in the Corbie Area.
Many decorations had been won and losses had been most severe. December was spent in holding the line in the same area but the Division was happily relieved on Christmas Eve and remained out until New Years Eve.

German retreat. The Companies were still in the same district when the enemy retired in March 1916, and they pursued him through Roquigny, Bus, Bertincourt, Ytres, Metz, and finally finished up at Havringcourt. It was during this action that No.217 (D) Coy. joined the Division and acted as the Divisional Company.

Nothing further of importance happened until the end of July, when the Division moved to Belgium after 3 weeks of training & recreation in the Candas Area.

Pilckem. "A" and "D" Coys. assisted the 38th Division in taking the Pilckem Ridge by putting over a heavy barrage of overhead fire. "D" Coy. lost their C.O. who was wounded, and Lieut.Lumm took command temporarily. One Section of H.Q. was in a pill-box which was square when they entered it, but after being hit 37 times it was made completely round. With most of these hits the men inside were knocked on the ground.

Steenbeck. On the 16-8-17 the M.G's working under the direction of Major H.B.Law who had been appointed D.M.G.O., fired a covering barrage to assist our infantry. "D" Coy. was commanded by Captain B.C. Parkinson-Cummine, and "C" Coy. by Captain DRYDURGH Casualties were heavy in all Coys. "D" Coy. lost 7 Officers out of 8, leaving only 14 men with 16 guns.

Eagle Trench. On 20-9-17, a similar action was fought in capturing Eagle Trench This was the hardest of all as the troops had occupied the line for some days under a constant barrage. Many decorations were won, Captain Odgers, commanding "A" Coy. was wounded, and afterwards awarded the M.C. "D" Coy. was commanded through this battle by Captain Rollings.

-2-

Cambrai. During our advance towards Cambrai on the 20-11-17, the M.G's first fired an overhead barrage and then advanced with the remainder of the Cavalry, Infantry and Tanks, with complete success as far as our troops went. They remained until the counter-attack on the 30-11-17. Many guns were hit and knocked out of action before the enemy came over, and the gun teams attached themselves to the infantry and used rifles. Captain Tanner, commanding "_" Coy. and his 3 Section Officers were killed. Only 17 men and the C.S.M. returned, the latter was awarded the D.C.M. "B" Coy. received 5 M.C's, the other Coys. suffered in the same way and received similar awards.

After spending 6 weeks in the Menin Road Section at Ypres, the Division moved to the Ercheu Area and here the Battalion was formed. The official date was 23rd February, but it was not until March 15th that the Battalion was complete. The increase in personnel was formed by drafts from all Infantry Battalions in the Division. 59th, 60th, and 61st Coys. became A, B, and C, and 217th became D Coy. Order of Battle was :-

Commanding   Lt. Col. H.L.Riley, D.S.O.
2nd in Command. Major. H.B. Law.
Adjutant.   Captain A.M.Crompton.
Quartermaster. Lieut.& Qr.Mr. F.J.Cooper.
Battn. Transport Officer. Captain A.E.F.Hill, M.C.

Company Commanders.
"A" Coy.   Major A.N. Richardson, M.C.
"B" Coy.   Major.B.D. Parkinson-Cumwine, MC.
"C" Coy.   Major W.L.Lewett, M.C.
"D" Coy.   Major A.L. Rollings, M.C.

The German offensive was imminent at this time and on March 20th we were packed up ready to move. Surplus Kit was stored at Libermont, and that was the last that was ever seen of it. "B" Coy. joined 60th Bde. at Ham on the evening of 20th March, and "A" and "C" joined 59th and 61st Bdes. on the morning of 21st. "D" Coy.(Divisional Reserve) and Battn. H.qrs. moved to Aubigny. During the subsequent fighting "A", "B", and "C" Coys. were working with their respective Brigades, nothing being seen of "C" Coy, for several days as the 61st Infantry Brigade was detached from the Division and were with the 36th Division. This Company was commanded throughout by Captain L.C. McLearon. Space does not allow of any detailed account of the 10 days' fighting, but particularly fine targets were secured by "A" Coy at BETHENCOURT, and by a mixed detachment, assisted by a Canadian Motor Battery, at HOMBLEUX.

When the Division was finally relieved, the Battalion moved back by lorry and route march to MERS, which was reached on April 14th and a draft of 12 Officers and 200 O.R. joined us at LE TRANSLAY on the march down. The final Day's march was a long one, very hot, and the Battalion halted for 6 hours about 7 miles from MERS as it was doubtful if we should be allowed to billet there, the town being out of the Divisional Area. We finally marched in just before dusk, and had a great reception, nearly the whole population turning out. 2 Companies were billeted in the CASINO and 2 at the Ordnance Depot, subsequently moving to the Hospice. The Officers were accommodated in 2 hotels which were entirely at our disposal. We had an excellent time during the week that we were at MERS, and everyone was very kind to us, the French Commandant going specially out of his way to help us on all occasions. A number of mules had their first experience of sea bathing; unfortunately the weather was cold, but a few men bathed one day to the great interest of the people on the promenade. On April 21st we entrained and arrived next day at CAMBLIGNEUL, where we remained for about a fortnight. Our stay here was chiefly noticeable for P.U.O. which struck down most of the Battalion. From here we marched up and took over the LENS SECTOR from the Canadians, 3 companies being in the line in 2 groups, and 1 company and Battn.H.Q. in a very good camp at MARQUEFFLES FARM, just North of NOTRE DAME DE LORETTE Spur. The remainder of the Division was on the S. side of the Hill, in the SOUCHEZ Valley, about 6 miles away by road. We thought that we had got a permanent home, but the Canadians coming up into close support, we had to move again, and found ourselves at SCOTTS CAMP

CARENCY, a collection of small sheds, with, however, excellent transport lines. We eventually made ourselves quite comfortable one of the chief drawbacks being the absence of any recreation ground, except on the hill in view of the German Lines. Another unpleasantness was the almost nightly arrival of German bombing planes. Fortunately they were generally bent on going further afield, and our camp was left alone.

The LENS SECTOR was very quiet during our time there, with the exception of periodical concentrations of gas shell; indeed, during September, the line was safer than the camp, as an H.V. gun started shelling the camp, usually between 11 p.m. and midnight. Several duds fell in the camp, and we were very fortunate in having only 2 casualties from this gun; but it necessitated an almost nightly exodus to trenches and banks, the animals also had to be taken clear of the camp every night.

On relief by the 12th Battn. M.G.C. at the beginning of October, we moved by bus to LA THIEULOYE. We put in a lot of training here and also very successful Battalion Sports, which were won by "D" Company. A lot of football was played, both Battalion matches and inter-company and inter-section competitions. A small theatre was lent to us by the R.E. workshops, about a mile from our billets and the Concert Party, the "Spare Parts", who had just been formed at CARENCY made rapid progress.

From here we moved to the CAMBRAI FRONT, and finally found ourselves on Armistice day on the MONS- MAUBEUGE ROAD. After a few days at FEIGNIES we moved back to MARIEUX where those of us who have not been demobilized, still remain. Several Football grounds are available and a number of matches have been played. The Battalion Team reached the Semi-final of the Inter-Battalion competition when snow put an end to everything. There is an excellent theatre at this place, formerly a Corps Cinema, and this was entirely XXXXXXXX fitted with electric light and the scenery made and painted by members of the Battalion. The "Spare Parts" gave a number of excellent shows, and the theatre was invariably packed whenever they performed. They also toured round the Division, and assisted by two artistes from the 61st Field Ambulance, who were the only other troops in MARIEUX, established a great reputation. Lieut. Davies was very largely responsible for the success achieved, and he was assisted very much by Major Law, who collected some wonderful dresses for the ladies, even finding it necessary to visit PARIS at frequent intervals to see the latest models.

20th Divisional M.Gs.

Battalion formed 15.3.18 from 59th-60th-61st
and 217th M.G.Cos.
-)))---------------------------------

20th BATTALION

MACHINE GUN C̶O̶MPANY BN

MARCH 1918

Army Form C. 2118.

WAR DIARY
or
INTELLIGENCE SUMMARY.
(Erase heading not required)

20th Bn. M.G.C.

Place	Date	Hour	Summary of Events and Information	Remarks and references to Appendices
LIBERMONT.	15th March		Batt. H.Q. formed. Lieut A.M. CROMPTON and Lieut A.E.F. HILL, M.C. took on duties of Adjutant and Transport officer respectively. Sq. Coy, 61st Coy, 61st Jt. Coy & 217th d Coy became A. B. C. & D Coys. Battn. up to strength with exception of 3 officers & Signal section R.E.: 170 men had recently been transferred for 3 months & were only partially trained. Major H.B. LAW returned from M.G. School CAMIERS and took over duties of 2nd in Command. It was decided that Companies should go into action with 6 officers & 130 O.R. exclusive of Transport.	
	16th		Party of officers & N.C.O's from A. & D. Coys reconnoitred Rear Zone position. B. & C. Coys practised a Scheme, taking up defensive position.	
	17th		Battn. Church Parade. 60th Bn. B.L. Horse Show	
	18th		Party of officers & N.C.O's from B. & C. Coys reconnoitred Rear Zone position. A. & D. Coys practised scheme, taking up defensive position. B. & C. Coys shooting on Range	
	19th		Party of officers & N.C.O's from B. & D. Coys reconnoitred Rear Zone position. & going over all Coys shooting on Range & practising changing position with Lewis hun + backwards & over	

WAR DIARY
or
INTELLIGENCE SUMMARY.

Army Form C. 2118.

Place	Date	Hour	Summary of Events and Information	Remarks and references to Appendices
LIBERMONT	20th		Packed up & stood officers kits, blankets & packs (less greatcoats). Warning order of probable German attack.	
		4 pm	B Coy under Capt PARKINSON CUMMINS M.C. marched to HAM & joined 60th Bn Gnrt.	By not from Sheet 66d
			D Coy (2 section)	
	21st		Heavy bombardment on whole front started in early morning.	
		9-30 am	C Coy under Lieut McLAREN marched to FRENICHES & joined 61st Bn Gnrt.	
		12 non	A " under Lieut HOWARD marched to OGNOLLES & joined 59th Bn Gnrt.	
		2 pm	Battn H.Q. & D Coy (less 1 section) marched to AUBIGNY arriving there 6-30 P.M. & went into billets in Div reserve.	
			During the afternoon the 3 Brigades went into battle in the Rear Zone of Defence.	
			B & C Coy took up previously arranged positions in rear zone of Lynes during the night.	
			A " " " " " " " " " " " " early on 22nd March	
			D. Coy in Reserve in AUBIGNY with Bn H.Q.	
	22nd		A Coy. Orders were received for 2 sections to concentrate at FORESTE. 6 guns under at 6 P.M.	
			2/Lt TOKE whilst approaching GERMAINE were suddenly fired on by M.G. at close range, nearly all the team became casualties, 5 men with one gun eventually escaping.	Mt Rubus Hill

Army Form C. 2118.

WAR DIARY
or
INTELLIGENCE SUMMARY.
(Erase heading not required)

Instructions regarding War Diaries and Intelligence Summaries are contained in F. S. Regs., Part II. and the Staff Manual respectively. Title pages will be prepared in manuscript.

Place	Date	Hour	Summary of Events and Information	Remarks and references to Appendices
		9 P.m. to midnight	Remaining guns took up positions on the DOUILLY – CROIX-MOLIGNAUX Line. 1 gun N. of VAUX fired several shells at range of 200 yds at German advancing in extended order in large numbers at 4 P.m.	
Coy H.Q. DOUILLE				
B. Coy.			In position in Rear Zone of Defence. Several attacks N.N.W. of HAPPENCOURT were repulsed during morning & early afternoon. at about 3 P.m. 30th & 36th Divns withdrew from battle zone through the 60th Bde. The 30th Divn was closely followed by the enemy, who broke through near FLUQUIERES, at the same time advancing down the VAUX valley beyond the flank of the 60th Bde. Heavy casualties were inflicted on the Germans, but at the point of penetration 2 guns were destroyed & their jus at the beginning of the attack. The 60th Bde. fell back to the line E. of MILL WOOD (L.1.a) & subsequently to prepared line E. of BRAY-ST-CHRISTOPHE – AUBIGNY – VILLERS ST CHRISTOPHE. 2 guns of D Coy which were sent up at a gallop came into action E. of MILL WOOD & fired 16 belts onto the Western exits from FLUQUIERES. A party of Germans who had crossed the St QUENTIN CANAL at TUGNY about 7 P.m. attacked BRAY ST CHRISTOPHE from S.W. & S.E., getting behind 60th Inf. Bde. who	10th R. Dub. Fus
		11 P.m		

WAR DIARY
or
INTELLIGENCE SUMMARY.
(Erase heading not required.)

Place	Date	Hour	Summary of Events and Information	Remarks and references to Appendices
			were holding Eastern exits of AUBIGNY. There was a very thick mist at the time.	
			4 gun team took part in a counter attack organised by Lieut Col WELCH D.S.O. Comdg 6th K.O.L.I.	Sheet 56d
			& eventually withdrew with the K.S.L.I. during morning of 23rd.	
			Remaining guns withdrew with 6th & 9th Bn behind HAM defences, eventually concentrating at HAM.	
			C Coy Orders were received at 3am 22nd to withdraw from ST SIMON Bridgehead to W bank of the ST QUENTIN CANAL. This was completed by 9am.	
			Disposition. 4 guns west (2) of Ken's opposite TOGNY (2 of these were destroyed by shell fire during the day)	
			4 " " J Somme LINE of ANNOIS	
			4 " on high ground E of DRURY-OLLEZY Road	
			4 " " " N of OLLEZY-ST SIMON Road.	
			At 7 P.m Enemy crossed the Canal near TUGNY. The infantry & 8 guns took up position on S. side of Canal along FLAVY - HAM railway.	
	10a.m		D Coy	M.F.Rutherford Major
			4 guns posted 1000yds S of BRAY ST CHRISTOPHE to cover right flank of 60th BDE.	
			2 " in position of readiness 500yds W of BRAY ST CHRISTOPHE	
			2 " in position at HILL 85 (L-15-c). These 2 guns fired a number of belts at parties of enemy trying to work along the canal bank during the afternoon.	

Army Form C. 2118.

WAR DIARY
or
INTELLIGENCE SUMMARY.
(Erase heading not required.)

Place	Date	Hour	Summary of Events and Information	Remarks and references to Appendices
	22	3 p.m.	4 guns in position outside ST QUENTIN - HAM Road 500 N.E. of AUBIGNY to support proposed counter attack of 5·9 & 9·4 B.L. in Southerly direction. 2 of these guns were sent forward at a gallop to MILL WOOD to check advance of Germans from FLUQUIERES	
		5 p.m.		sheet 66d
		7.30 p.m.	2 guns took up position at N.E. corner of VILLERS ST CHRISTOPHE to cover, got between 60d. 59 b1 Ptb	
		8.30 p.m.	2 guns to railway crossing 800 S.W. of AUBIGNY on main road. 2 " to forked roads IK.15 central.	
	23	midnight 1 a.m.	Germans attacked AUBIGNY from S.S.E. & a considerable number got into the village & began to advance down the HAM Road. They were completely checked by close range fire from the 2 guns on the railway crossing & retired into the village. These 2 guns remained in position until all troops & guns had retired, when the withdrew unmolested about 3 a.m.	H.G. Riley Major

Army Form C. 2118.

WAR DIARY
or
INTELLIGENCE SUMMARY.
(Erase heading not required.)

Place	Date	Hour	Summary of Events and Information	Remarks and references to Appendices
	23rd		A Coy. All guns were ordered to withdraw behind CANAL DE LA SOMME & were in position from BETHENCOURT to VOYENNES (inclusive) by dawn 23rd.	
		9 a.m.	12 horsemen rode over the ridge at VILLECOURT & were fired on by 2 guns; a few minutes late 10 riderless horses came down the hill towards the canal.	
			About 2 companies of infantry in extended order followed the horsemen, & behind them small bodies of men, mostly Right M.G. teams. These were engaged with excellent results.	
			Then 2 guns were kept busy most of the day firing at the enemy who made repeated attempts to get down the slopes to the canal. Very heavy casualties were inflicted & all advances stopped.	
		4 p.m.	Heavy shelling along canal banks opposite VOYENNES until dark.	
		midnight	Heavy intermittent shelling again opened on canal bank.	
		3 p.m.	2 guns at J-7-d-5-1, just E of VOYENNES observed 3 or 4 horsemen & a wagon on the opposite slopes. Fire was opened & the wagon was checked, & the casualties being inflicted.	
			2 guns were destroyed by shell fire during the night.	H.E.Riley Major

WAR DIARY
or
INTELLIGENCE SUMMARY.
(Erase heading not required)

Place	Date	Hour	Summary of Events and Information	Remarks and references to Appendices
	23rd	2 pm	**C. Coy** 6 guns on the FLAVY HAM Railway were continually in action from 10 a.m. till dusk, when they were ordered to withdraw S of the Railway. Some good targets were obtained. There were a number of casualties among the teams, as they were subjected to rifle fire + shrapnel fire from the right rear, where the Germans were advancing from JUSSY. 4 guns were attached to K.R.S.R (36th Div) & took up positions SW of CUGNY. These were withdrawn with the evening to positions E of VILLESELVE. 4 guns between EAUCOURT & CUGNY.	Sket 6 & d.
			at midnight 9 guns were in action. The guns were ready all in action throughout the day, the fire in the western country S of CUGNY being at close range. **B & D Coy** By dawn 8 guns were in position covering the road crossings between COURTEMANCHE and CANIZY. When the mist lifted sufficiently 5 guns were left near the road crossings, 3 placed in action. Position 300× N of railway in J.19 + J.36. 4 guns were kept in reserve S of railway. 2 guns opposite OFFOY destroyed several parties of Germans moving about in OFFOY during the afternoon.	M.G. Coy 1104

Army Form C. 2118.

WAR DIARY
or
INTELLIGENCE SUMMARY.
(Erase heading not required.)

Date	Hour	Summary of Events and Information	Remarks and references to Appendices
23rd	2 pm	2 guns moved from J.26 to railway about J.33.b between S.W. exits from CANIZY & railway to the S.E. B:H.Q. Factory N.E. of HOMBLEUX.	
24th		A Coy. Early morning considerably quiet until daylight when successful attempt was made by the Germans to get a man at the canal at BETHENCOURT N of it. Attempts attack BETHENCOURT all lights down with heavy loss, but at about 10-30 a.m. enemy crossed the canal N of BETHENCOURT (8th Div front) & filed into the back of the 2 guns at BETHENCOURT from C-22-central. 2/Lt HEWETT & 2 Sgt (Crofoot) & 9 men of the two teams, 2/Lt HEWETT was wounded. Sergeant kept his gun in action during 5 casualties. 2/Lt HEWETT and his team at front flank range & causing enormous casualties. They expended all their ammunition & withdrew when the Germans were within 50y, first disabling the gun.	
	9 am	1 gun was moved from ROUY-LE-GRAND to I-11-b-2-3. 2 guns manned by details from LEDERMONT of all corps, took up position between I-12-a-0-1 & I-12-a-9-1; the remaining guns of the personnel acting as infantry to refill the canal bank to the North.	1st Rly Hg
	11-30 am	Remaining guns on Canal bank attempt to VOYENNES, 1 on gun at I-12-c-9-1 [illegible] this gun 2 KG guns.	

WAR DIARY
INTELLIGENCE SUMMARY

Army Form C. 2118.

Place	Date	Hour	Summary of Events and Information	Remarks and references to Appendices
	24	11-45 a.m.	Infantry withdraw.	
		12 noon	Behind of gun team with one gun withdrew to MAM NEUFS Road I-16-c, where they were joined by Coy H.Q. & the only remaining gun. At dusk these guns were placed in position at I-15-c-2-7 and I-21-b-2-9 attached to 2nd Scottish Rifles.	
			C. Coy.	
		10 a.m.	Heavy attack No 3 of VILLESELVE, drawing back on banks; 2 guns < from loss. 2 guns took up position just N of VILLESELVE – BEUVEN Road & fired on enemy who were trying to outflank from a wood N of VILLESELVE with excellent results. The cavalry then charged the ridge, & infantry must forced forward supported by 2 M.G. They were eventually forced to retire & while holding the ridge then 2 guns took up position behind an east side of the BUCHOIR – BERLANCOURT Road.	Capt. G.S.L.
		8 p.m.	Soon after dusk these guns were withdrawn & took up position along the sunken roads N.N.N. – GUISCARD Road, just N. of ST MARTIN, together with infantry of various regiments. 4 guns remained intact.	1st Rly. M.G.

WAR DIARY or INTELLIGENCE SUMMARY

Army Form C. 2118.

Place	Date	Hour	Summary of Events and Information	Remarks and references to Appendices
	24		B.D Corps	
		8 a.m	At about 8 a.m an attack developed along the Railway embankment from HAM, & also from CANIZY. The latter attack was stopped by 2 M.G. on the railway on J-7-d-7-0-0. 66 d. A counter attack by 12th R.R. & (the enemy retired into CANIZY.	
		9 a.m	Further the attack succeeded in moving its railway on J-35-A-6 & 9 a.m had occupied the bridge over the S[t]am at J-34-b-6-2 & the next running at J-34-b-0-4.	
			Further to the south, the Division were again in falling back rapidly & by about 11-30 a.m the greater part of EIMERY HALLON appeared to be occupied by the enemy. Several attempts to advance along the railway & from CANIZY were stopped by 14th R.R. and 4 M.G. on its railway in front of being eighty guns.	
		11 a.m	At about 11 a.m. 83rd Field Cy R.E. moved up & took up a position on the S. western edge of HILL 70 (J-72-b-2-d)	
		11-45 a.m	4 guns of Canadian Motor M.G.B. arrived & 2 guns were placed in HOMBLEUX Cemetery & 2 in redoubt about J-32-A-4-0	H.Q Relay H.Q
		12-30 p.m	Germans were apparently GRECOURT from the S.E & E. Two guns from armoured cars sent to take up a position just S of HOMBLEUX & Salinguent & other S.W of HOMBLEUX.	

WAR DIARY
or
INTELLIGENCE SUMMARY
(Erase heading not required.)

Army Form C. 2118.

Place	Date	Hour	Summary of Events and Information	Remarks and references to Appendices
	24th	4-M?	The 4 gun stopped & sought attempts by small parties of Germans to envelop HOMBLEUX from the S.; a large number of Germans collected behind the wood in Q-8-d-, but did not advance under the whirring of other Infantry were in prepare the attempt was checked by the 4 guns, destroyed parts of attack got within 300x of HOMBLEUX.	
		2-30 p.m	Infantry commenced withdrawing behind LIBERMONT – BACQUENCOURT Canal. Holding posts in town of 2 of 6 guns on the Railway in J-26-d, but they were still firing for a considerable time after all the Infantry had retired.	
		3 p.m	Germans advanced in large numbers down the HAM-NESLE Road, arriving in J-26-d, from E & S; through J-32, P 1 & 2. The 4 Canadian guns, 2 guns at southern end for HOMBLEUX & a gun mounted in the upper storey of the factory at J-31-a-5-5- got some excellent targets shortly on the HAM-NESLE Road when the enemy advanced in mass, as guns fired several belts at ranges between 800x & 300x, inflicting very heavy losses.	
		3-4 p.m	The R.E.s of the attack until all hope had arrived the canal, when they gradually withdrew covered by 2 guns in Eastern outskirts of BACQUENCOURT & 2 guns S.W. of HOMBLEUX. The German R.E. lengths of period M.G. on to HILL 70 - opened heavy fire on HOMBLEUX. A number of casualties were sustained, but only 1 gun was lost.	H.P. Riley Major

WAR DIARY
or
INTELLIGENCE SUMMARY.
(Erase heading not required.)

Army Form C. 2118.

Place	Date	Hour	Summary of Events and Information	Remarks and references to Appendices
		4-10 p.	about ½ hour after HAMBLEUX had been captured received the German orders from an OR with OC Coys 2 Battalion - directed it gave ½ hour P.m. had orders to go in trenches	
		4-30 p.m	all guns west of BACQUENCOURT Canal owing to being pushed back on to the PERONNE-QUESNEL Distribution	
			3 guns Canadian south in G.C. covering BACQUENCOURT Bridge	
			2 guns covering Canal at QUIVERY	
			2 " " " " BUVERCHY	
			4 " on bend of road between LANGUEVOISIN and MOYENCOURT	
			5 " in PLESSIER E of CRECY, one gun	
			B.H.Q. CRECY	
	25th	8 a.m	A Coy Lieut HOWARD with remainder of Coy acted as Infantry, also taking over stragglers from different Regiments East and Division - took up a position on a trench in H.35 a & b facing N.E. During the afternoon sent found troops after detach jus back for direction of HEILY and protect the Cars for the night.	
		10 p.m	Major BERTIE 11 - R.B. took over command of all its details plus	H.Q.Rly/14

WAR DIARY
or
INTELLIGENCE SUMMARY.

Army Form C. 2118.

Place	Date	Hour	Summary of Events and Information	Remarks and references to Appendices
	25/4		C. Coy to ____ _____ _____ from ____ _____ ____ _____ ____	
			Remaining 4 guns joined 6th Bde. Aftr[?] pass ANZICOURT at 3 P.m. and at 3.30 P.m entrained evening near GAUNY at 6.30 p.m. Position was taken up behind the wire on the line LIANCOURT-FOSSE — CREMERY?. _____ _____ _____ _____ _____	
			B. D. Coy.	
		11 a.m	In consequence of the advance of the enemy through NESLE reserve guns were moved to _____	
			2 guns x roads I-25-d-0-1 [?]	
			2 " Forked Roads 0-1-b-3-2.	
		3 p.m.	Tenth of Bn. H.Q. Div. and other details (incl. Lewis gun M.G. from QUIQUERY & I-25 retired 2 km during the day, the new position being _____ against _____ again. The 2 guns at I-25-d-0-1 were left installed [?] for an hour or two in reserve, but could see no German within 2000 yards. all our batteries had withdrawn, but a French 75 mm took up a position in CRESSY remained in action throughout the afternoon.	Shute 66 d
		4 p.m	30th Div. on our right retired from MOYENCOURT	
			Remaining 2 reserve guns moved to 0-3-c S.E. of CRESSY to form defensive flank to S.S.E. 2 guns from 0-3 central to 0-9-a to secure this flank.	H. Riley Hts.
		5 p.m	_____ _____ _____	

Army Form C. 2118.

Army Form C. 2118.

WAR DIARY
or
INTELLIGENCE SUMMARY.
(Erase heading not required.)

Instructions regarding War Diaries and Intelligence Summaries are contained in F.S. Regs., Part II. and the Staff Manual respectively. Title pages will be prepared in manuscript.

Place	Date	Hour	Summary of Events and Information	Remarks and references to Appendices
	25th	5.30 am	Infantry attacked. Several hundreds from various divisions were collected on the road N.W. of CRESSY & part of it from different platoons to N. between CRESSY and BILLANCOURT. Enemy guns fired several shells after infantry had passed through & were concentrated at CRESSY.	
		8.30 pm	Disposition of guns 2 on road 0.3.c.1.4 S.E. of CRESSY 2 " " 0.7.b.9.4 E " " 2 " " 0.1.b.3.3 N " " 2 " arty H.36.c.5.9 N " of BILLANCOURT 2 " Inft. H.35.d.9.9 N " " 2 " " H.34.d.1.4 N.E. of RETHONVILLERS 2 " guns B. A.Q. BIARRE 3 guns Canadian M.M.G.C. en route for BIARRE	
		10 pm	There was a good deal of confusion & activity in the Northern outskirts of BILLANCOURT. 2 or 3 attempts were made by the Germans along the Roads leading from N.E. & N.W. 2 guns & teams were lost with exception of 2 wounded men.	

14 Feby 1918

WAR DIARY
or
INTELLIGENCE SUMMARY.
(Erase heading not required.)

Army Form C. 2118.

Place	Date	Hour	Summary of Events and Information	Remarks and references to Appendices
	25th	11-30 p	about 11-30 pm orders received for Divn. to concentrate at ROYE, NE of village	
		2-30 p	All guns of B&D Coys concentrated at BEAERE by 2-30 pm & marched thro' BALATRE on CARREPUIS & E. outskirts of ROYE where they were joined by remainder of A Coy & halted for 2 hours. Received 2 to extra 2 spare 4 tubes & was 2/6" screw.	
		1-30 p	Canadian M.M.Q.E. provided day limits and sent to report at ROYE.	
			4 guns A Coy E Exped at FLIES	
			4 " B " E " A " ARVILLERS	
	26th		"C" Coy, acting as infantry, moved until 6.15 A.M. as flank guard to remainder of Division & rejoined Battn. at LE QUESNEL. LE QUESNEL DEFENCE	
		6 a.m	A.B.D.Coys & B" H.Q. been up A L C Coys with Rd. was acting as guard of A & C Coys under Lt. Col. Geslin as guard to the Division until 2 Coys 12th K.R.R. Battn acted as rear guard to the Division until 2 Coys 12th K.R.R. who had been relieved by delay in ROYEE while Division formed up & various details of the Division joined the Column. a few shells were fired at the column during the march, but did no damage. a lot of stragglers from various details were collected & brought along with the Rear Guard. Arrived LE QUESNEL about 12-30 p.m. Orders were received for 4 guns to move forward at	H.P.Riley Ltd

WAR DIARY
or
INTELLIGENCE SUMMARY

Army Form C. 2118.

(Erase heading not required.)

Place	Date	Hour	Summary of Events and Information	Remarks and references to Appendices
			Our forward posts reported enemy advancing on the villages. 6 Sent mounted orderlies & sent out an advance - at the same time to order for its 4 guns. Wire cancelled. M.M.G. sent instead. 16 new guns were received & 10 additional tripods; also 350 belt boxes. Full teams were found & following dispositions made:- 4 guns A. Coy. to 59th Bde at FOLIES. 4 " B " " 60th Bde at ARVILLERS. 4 " D " " 61st Bde at BEAUFORT. 7 " D & C in reserve positions in LE QUESNEL Defences. Late 8 further teams were found from men of A & C Coys who had been acting as injured for the past 3 days. Considerable delay caused by the fact that all the Battn Transport had been ordered out of the Wood when it had been packed, taking with it spare ammunition, oil & the new chargers. It was received after 1½ hours delay & 250 belt boxes filled. Quiet night. B = H.Q. LE QUESNEL	Feb 1918

WAR DIARY
or
INTELLIGENCE SUMMARY
(Erase heading not required.)

Army Form C. 2118.

Place	Date	Hour	Summary of Events and Information	Remarks and references to Appendices
	27th		Disposition as previous day: 4 guns between FOLIES and BEAUFORT, front 15-yards at 200° at flanks of enemy. These guns were subsequently moved forward E.S.E. of FOLIES to prevent enemy debouching from BOUCHOIR. They suffered some casualties from M.G. fire from trees in BOUCHOIR.	sheet 66 E
		3 P.M		
		6 P.M	2 extra guns of C Coy sent up E. of 59th Bn.	
	28th		During night 27/28th Division (less 60th M. Bde.) relieved by French & concentrated in wood S.of LE QUESNEL CHATEAU. Battn. collected with exception of B Coy (with 60th M Bde.)	
		7.30 a.m	Marched from LE QUESNEL across country in artillery formation, an enemy was shelling the main ROYE–AMIENS Road with hollow observation. no casualties.	
		12 noon	Halted for dinner in wood on N. side of ROYE–AMIENS Road. C–18–b. 2 guns in position on high ground N.W. of wood C–12–b. Mounted scouts out on ridge N.E. of MEZIERES D–8–b.	
		7 P.M	61st Bde. occupied line from DEMUIN to N.W. of MEZIERES D–20–a. Guns were disposed as follows: 4 guns on high ground between MAISON BLANCHES – COURCELLES.	H.Pulley W.H.

WAR DIARY
or
INTELLIGENCE SUMMARY.
(Erase heading not required.)

Army Form C. 2118.

Place	Date	Hour	Summary of Events and Information	Remarks and references to Appendices
	28		1 gun Flagholds ROYE-AMIENS Road D-14-c & D-20-a covering western exits from MAISON	flank
			BLANCHE and MEZIERES.	66 E
			3 guns between MEZIERES and VILLERS AUX ERABLES watching right flank.	
			2" C-24 central covering right flank & exits from VILLERS AUX ERABLE.	
			2" Hof ground S.W of DEMUIN C-12-a. watching left flank.	
			4 " activity ROYE-AMIENS Road D-13-a & C-18-d covering exits from wood	
			in D-13-b&d.	
			Bt H.Q. C-18-b-8-6.	
	29	6 a.m.	3 guns moved from D-20-a&b to N.E of MEZIERES D-21-c. 2 guns from reserve sent up to D-20-a.	
			From 10 a.m to about 12-30 p.m. Germans in small parties tried repeatedly to advance along both sides of the ROYE-AMIENS ROAD. A number of belts were found at ranges between 600 & 1000 y. Single men crawling forward to closer range had to be engaged, as no one else was firing.	H.D by 7 H
		12-30 p.m	Enemy withdrew from MEZIERES	

Army Form C. 2118.

WAR DIARY
or
INTELLIGENCE SUMMARY.
(Erase heading not required.)

Instructions regarding War Diaries and Intelligence Summaries are contained in F. S. Regs., Part II. and the Staff Manual respectively. Title pages will be prepared in manuscript.

Place	Date	Hour	Summary of Events and Information	Remarks and references to Appendices
	29	2-30pm	A good deal of movement observed near MEZIERES CEMETERY.	65 E
		3-30pm	Germans observed to be reinforcing behind MAISON BLANCHE.	
		4 P.M	About 200 Germans advanced from MAISON BLANCHE and BRICKFIELD 300 x at the most. These were caught at very close range by 3 guns & lost very heavily. The few survivors retired. A counter attack of the 60th Bde penetrated MEZIERES but the enemy were soon round this right flank & also held the high ground in D-15-a-+- the whole line retired to a line running roughly from DEMUIN - X roads C-11-d - C-22-b. 4 guns just out of action & 4 lost during the afternoon & evening.	
		7-30pm	Lt HILL + in command of 4 guns astride main road in D-13-a and C-18-d went forward to reconnoitre. Situation in wood D-13-b+d after the infantry had retired x was not seen again.	
		9pm	There was a lot of confused fighting on the edge of the wood on both sides of the road in D-13-a and front C-18-d. One gun and 4 men eventually got back to our new line.	# 7 aby 7 W.
	30	9 a.m.	Distribution. 7 guns & 8 guns of 5th Div. along line of road from DEMUIN & C-22-b. of 12th Bde C-11-a-6-6. 2 guns C-16-b-8-8.	

WAR DIARY
or
INTELLIGENCE SUMMARY.
(Erase heading not required.)

Army Form C. 2118.

Place	Date	Hour	Summary of Events and Information	Remarks and references to Appendices
			2 guns C-16-C-3-5	66 E.
			2 recent guns about A of HANGARD. (Amiens map)	Amiens map
			During the morning 4 more guns were moved - 2 of them were placed at C-8-6-1-9, and 2	66. E.
			kept in reserve position. Not DOMART.	
			Throughout the day there was intermittent shelling & a good deal of movement on both sides & patterns	
			of the line advancing and retiring. No targets of any importance presented themselves, but	
			a gun just S.W. of DEMUIN fired several bursts with visible effect at parties crossing a gap	
			between Woods in DEMUIN & also fired in support of a small counterattack by French Troops	
			About 3-30 p.m. our troops retired from LITTLE WOOD which was occupied by the enemy, but retaken	
			about 7 p.m. by the 66th Bde.	
		31	Night of 30th/31st was quiet.	
		5 a.m.	2 guns were moved from vicinity of X roads C-11-d to S.W. of RIFLE WOOD C-16-b-2-7.	
			to watch valley running up to E-17-C.	
		12.30 p.m.	Heavy shelling of C-16 and C-22-b followed by attack on CAVALRY WOOD. A number	A.P. Rly / Hd.
			of bells were fired at Germans advancing in C-23-a & c, but trench mortar observation	
			of fire very difficult. One gun destroyed by shell fire & one reduced to single shots	

Army Form C. 2118.

WAR DIARY
or
INTELLIGENCE SUMMARY.
(Erase heading not required.)

Place	Date	Hour	Summary of Events and Information	Remarks and references to Appendices
	31	2.30 p.m.	Troops on our right were retiring from CAVALRY WOOD & our right flank was withdrawn to conform, encircling LITTLE WOOD.	
		3.30 p.m.	Enemy were holding the Northern edge of CAVALRY WOOD & were working down the Eastern ground in C.16-c.2.d.	
			The 4 guns in C.16-c & C.16-b fired all their ammunition & 2 eventually repaired during the night.	
			At about 4 p.m. 3 guns who were still holding their post in small infantry posts were caught by our barrage & suffered several casualties. Only 1 of these guns on C.11-d were caught by our barrage & suffered several casualties. Only 1 of these guns got back, & attacked they & a party of 6th K.S.L.I. who were holding a line in C.10-a.	
			During the evening & night 2 guns were placed at the Bridge-Head at HOOGE.	
			7 guns were in position S of St. Rue LUCE	
			8 " " " N " " LUCE	
				H R Riley 1/Lt
				H R Riley 1/Lt
				Cmdg 20th Bn. M.G.C.

Army Form C. 2118.

WAR DIARY
or
INTELLIGENCE SUMMARY.
(Erase heading not required.)

Place	Date	Hour	Summary of Events and Information	Remarks and references to Appendices
	1918			
FARM HOUSE (Sheet 62.D) 7.20 A.B.10.	Apr 1st	3.am	The Battalion moved from Farm House (Sheet 62.D) 7.20 A. 95.10. and occupied billets in RUM&IANL S.W. AMIENS (Sheet AMIENS.17)	
		2nd	Lists of Casualties compiled, also deficiencies in equipment and gear.	
		3rd	Battalion moved & went into billets NAMPS AU MONT and rejoined billets with HR and the shelter	
		4th & 5th	Reorganizing Battalion, cleaning and training under O.C. Coys.	
		7th	Battalion moved & took over from Battalion on Bois BRULE.	
		8th	Training continued. Lectures to Officers by P.S.O.I. 20th Divn on atmosphere. Batt.	
Sheet BOYON 10.		9th	Company training continued. C.O. British Patrols	
		10th	Battn. complete with transport arrived at BIENCOURT (Sheet 31E&F 14) (h.Q. Coys to k Patrol. Reinforcements from Base officers 12 officers 199 OR	
		11th	Chateau Battn & transport moved to MERS LES BAINS. The Staff Magazine (Sheet ABBEVILLE 12)	
SHACHABBEVILLE	12/13th		Organizing & cleaning up under O.C. Coys.	
	14th		Church Services. Springs ranks.	
	15/16th		Training under O.C. Coys. One Coy found on range each day. 3 officers & 28 NCOs &	
	17th		Training under O.C. Coys.	
	18/19		Battn. transport moved to GAMBLIGNEUL (Sheet LENS 12)	

Ull Cunifolon
Capt & Adjt

Army Form C. 2118.

WAR DIARY
or
INTELLIGENCE SUMMARY.
(Erase heading not required.)

Instructions regarding War Diaries and Intelligence Summaries are contained in F. S. Regs., Part II. and the Staff Manual respectively. Title pages will be prepared in manuscript.

Place	Date	Hour	Summary of Events and Information	Remarks and references to Appendices
Brit LENS II	20th		Training under O.C. Coys.	
	21st		Church Service for all ranks	
	22nd		Bathing. Training in accordance with Training Programme. Firing on range	
	23/24		Training. Firing on range	
	25th		Training. Lectures by Divisional Gunnery Officer to all officers & with the 21st June trench records.	
	26th/27th		Training as per programme	
	28th		Church Service for all ranks	
	29th/30th		Training. Firing on range	

W.M. Grant Capt. Adj.

Army Form C. 2118.

20th M.G. Bn
Vol 3

WAR DIARY
or
INTELLIGENCE SUMMARY.
(Erase heading not required.)

Instructions regarding War Diaries and Intelligence Summaries are contained in F.S. Regs., Part II. and the Staff Manual respectively. Title pages will be prepared in manuscript.

Place	Date 1918	Hour	Summary of Events and Information	Remarks and references to Appendices
CAMBLIGNEUL (Sheet LENS 11)	May 1		Machine Gun instruction and practice, including gun drill, indirect fire, fire control, musketry and elementary bombing.	
	2nd		Battn Transport moved to MARQUEFFLES FARM with the exception of 16 guns of "A" Coy & 10 guns of "C" Coy, which took up a position in rear of the 3rd Canadian Division Front. N.Y. SOUCHEZ RIVER, and formed the Left Group. H.Q. M.23.c. 25.30. (Sheet 36.c. S.W.L.) 2/Lt C.K. MOORE Joined as Signalling Officer.	
MARQUEFFLES FARM (Sheet LENS 11)	3rd		M.G. of 3rd Canadian Division S. of SOUCHEZ RIVER and 1 M.G. of 4th Canadian Division (S.12.a.90.50) were relieved by 12 guns of "B" Coy and 4 of "C" Coy. These guns formed the Right Group with H.Q. at S.6.a.60.m (Sheet 36.c. S.W. 3) a sub-section of "D" Coy relieved a sub-section of "C" Coy.	
	4th		General Training for gunners at Rear H.Q., including firing on the range with M.G. and rifles.	
	5th		Church Parade.	
	6/8th		Training continued.	
	9.		Battn Transport moved to SCOTTS CAMP, CARENCY. Guns in the Line relieved and 6 more sent up, making 12 guns in the Line per Coy.	
SCOTTS CAMP CARENCY.	10/30th		Life in the sector carried out during this period. The average number of rounds fired each night on selected targets has been 23,600 rounds. Lieut M.E. JACKSON and Lieut G.R.H. BAILEY joined 18th Major P.T. CASHIN and Major A. HOLT joining 20th as Company Commanders. 5 & B Route Forecast 15th & 8 & Route 20th. 2/Lt E.A. DUTTON and 2/Lieut P.W. COWTAN joined Battn 30.5.18.	

A.M.Brompton. Capt Major
.... Lieut Colonel
Commanding 20th ... BG

Army Form C. 2118.

WAR DIARY
OF
INTELLIGENCE SUMMARY.
(Erase heading not required.)

Instructions regarding War Diaries and Intelligence Summaries are contained in F.S. Regs., Part II. and the Staff Manual respectively. Title pages will be prepared in manuscript.

20th BATTALION, MACHINE GUN CORPS.

Place	Date	Hour	Summary of Events and Information	Remarks and references to Appendices
Scott Camp	June 1		General training for section and of the line	
	2		wounded (3. s. R.) 2 O.Rs. Racey	
			Church parade	
CARENCY	3/5		General training for section and of the line	
Sec¹ X16d.4.4.	6		Training continued. 2 O.Rs. wounded (1 remaining on duty)	
	7		Training continued. 1 O.R. wounded. 22 O.R Reinforcements arrived from Base Depot	
	8		Battalion Horse Show held in Area adjoining camp (not HQ) 1 O.R. reinforcement from Base	
	9/12		Training continued from Base	
	13		Training continued. 1 O.R. wounded	
	14		Training continued. Lecture "ABLAIN ST NAZAIRE" (Sheet 44b) By 2nd Lieut Coe Garage NCO for officer Sergeants in K liaison between the RAF and the Infantry and Machine Gun Corps	
	15		21 Reinforcements arrived from Base Depot	
	16		Church Parade	
	17/20		Training continues. 10 Recoveries wounded 19½. 2nd Lts Alpheries return from hospital. 19. E.M.	
	21		Lieut J.R. Remington for Officer Sharp @ WAVRANS James and A.G. Thorne sent deputed to hospital for Officer Sharp @ WAVRANS (CALAIS) Shar. R 37 strength	

Army Form C. 2118.

WAR DIARY
or
INTELLIGENCE SUMMARY.
(Erase heading not required.)

20th BATTALION MACHINE GUN CORPS.

JUNE 1917

Place	Date	Hour	Summary of Events and Information	Remarks and references to Appendices
Scott Camp	22		Training continued.	
CARENCY. Sheet 36d. 4.4.25/30	23		Church parade. Lecture by Divisione Gas Officer.	
	24		Training continued. 10R from Base Depot. Lieut E.M.V.Rainey rejoined from Hospital 27.6.16	
			During the whole of the period the Barracks was in the line on Left & Right Section of Divisione from 49 guns were in the line. Inter-section reliefs have been carried out during the period night firing according to programme has taken place, the average number of rounds fired 21,200. New M.G. emplacements have been made and occupied in accordance with New Defensive Policy of XVIII Corps	
				M Crompton Capt MGC

20 Bn M.G. Corps
WDC 5

Army Form C. 2118.
SECRET
WAR DIARY or INTELLIGENCE SUMMARY.
(Erase heading not required.)

Place	Date	Hour	Summary of Events and Information	Remarks and references to Appendices
Scott Camp CAMIERS X16 a.4.4. (Sheet 9 pm B)	July 1		General training for arrivals of the draft	
	2		Night 1/2nd. Enemy Bn. shelling in Eype Scotch Place, 3 ORs killed, 15 OR wounded	
	3		3 ORs wounded. From 20th A.E.F. Hussars command relief of 2nd in command	
			2/B Coy. met with fatal accident explosion. 100 reinforcements	
	5		2 ORs wounded gassed	
	7		dispatch services for all ranks	
	8/12		Training continued	
	13		19 other reinforcements arrived from Base Depot	
	14		Church service for all. A.V.C. Inspn. report 65 from A.V.C. Base Depot	
	16		Lectures by Gen. Officer Comdg. on front line	
	18		1 OR reinforcement from 102nd Bn. C.	
	19		30 ORs Reinforcements from Base Depot	
	21		1 OR accidentally wounded	
	22		1 OR wounded	
	23		Camp Library opened	

SECRET

Army Form C. 2118.

WAR DIARY
or
INTELLIGENCE SUMMARY.
(Erase heading not required.)

Instructions regarding War Diaries and Intelligence Summaries are contained in F. S. Regs., Part II. and the Staff Manual respectively. Title pages will be prepared in manuscript.

Place	Date	Hour	Summary of Events and Information	Remarks and references to Appendices
Rests Camp OPPRENCY #16.H.4.6. (Sheet 44B)	1918 July	24	1 OR killed. 2 wounded (accidentally).	
		30	Battalion Inspected by Corps General.	
			During the whole of the period the Battalion was in the Line in Reserve Type Sector & Divisional Front. Intensive training was continued in the Rifle Pits Firing. Training plus New entries were during the period. The average number of rounds fired weekly by Lewis gunners being 14,95000	

A. M. Crawford
Captain & Adjutant
for Lieut Colonel
Commanding 20th Bn M.G.C.

WAR DIARY
or
INTELLIGENCE SUMMARY.

(Erase heading not required.)

Army Form C. 2118.

20th Bn. M.G.C.

Vol 6

Instructions regarding War Diaries and Intelligence Summaries are contained in F. S. Regs., Part II. and the Staff Manual respectively. Title pages will be prepared in manuscript.

Place	Date 1918	Hour	Summary of Events and Information	Remarks and references to Appendices
SCOTT'S CAMP, CARENCY (6 kms W of Mont St Eloi) B	1st		Lieut D.R. Thomas & 1 O.R. transferred to the Reinforcement Camp.	
	2/3		Transport of Division moved to the Line. Lieut Perrins to train to take over 1 officer (A/Lt) 5 Sgts, 6 Cpls, 8 gns & temporarily attached to 20th Bde M.G.C. for employment.	
	4		1 O.R. wounded - rifle.	
	6		1 O.R. reinforcement.	
	9			
	10.		3 O.R.'s wounded.	
	11		Church Service. (11th R.B.) 2/Lt Kirkland A.P.M. Carpenter's return.	
	14		'C' Coy 20th M.G. & relieved coys of the M.G.C. on ridge in 9.15 & relieved by 20th M.G. & moved to Mericourt Section on 25' squares lying on the section for Lens section & Divisional Reserve. 'B' Section 'A' Coy moved from Lens section to Divisional Reserve.	
	15		2/Lt Jamie & Denby, reporting from base.	
	18		Church Service. 2 O.R. wounded.	
	22		2/Lieut A.D. Wragg from Base Depot. Reinforcement. 'A' Coy relieved 'B' Coy — the AVION SECTION (Canada Group) on nights 24 & 25. 'B' Coy moved to Divisional Reserve. Major D.L. Henson M.C. took over command of Canada Group	

CONFIDENTIAL.　　　　　　　　　20th Battn. M. G. C. No. M.G. 2/923.

20th Division, "A".

　　　　　　　Herewith War Diary for September, 1918.

　　　　　　　　　　　　　　　　　　A. M. Crompton
　　　　　　　　　　　　　　　　　　Captain & Adjutant,
　　　　　　　　　　　　　　　　　　　for Major,
29th September, 1918.　　　Comdg. 20th Bn. Machine Gun Corps.

WAR DIARY or INTELLIGENCE SUMMARY

Army Form C. 2118.

Place	Date	Hour	Summary of Events and Information	Remarks and references to Appendices
SCOTT'S COMM CARENCY	August 1918 27		Cy 20th Bn M.G.C. relieved D Cy 20th Bn M.G.C. in LENS SECTION (PREFOCA) August 29/7/18. D Cy moved to Bruay and Reserve. B Cy 20th Bn M.G.C. relieved Cy of the M.G.C. in ACHEVILLE SECTION (Quiet) on 26th Division. Being now the Sections from 20th Division on frontage the Brigade as follows:— AVION SECTION (PREFOCA) — LEFT GROUP MERICOURT SECTION (South Hd) — CENTRE GROUP ACHEVILLE SECTION (ZIELONE) — RIGHT GROUP August 29/7/18 Major P.J. Carter assumed command.	
	29		D Cy relieves B Cy in ACHEVILLE SECTION with no comment B Cy moved to Right Group	
	30		During the month enemy was carried out much 5.4"-gunning and average an increase of 16,19 rounds per night. Enemy infantry was most at N.31.a.8 M.3.a.2.55.37. New emplacements (splinter proof) were made at 5.16.a.7 M.34.a.20.80. New guns HQ complete no emplacement at M.36.c.95 to inspect. Position very quiet in front.	

(signed)
Captain & Adjutant
20th Bn M.G.C.

(signed) Lieut Colonel
Commanding 20th Bn M.G.C.

WAR DIARY
or
INTELLIGENCE SUMMARY.
(Erase heading not required.)

20 Bn M.G. Corps
Vol. 7

Place	Date	Hour	Summary of Events and Information	Remarks and references to Appendices
SCOTT'S CAMP CARENCY X16.d.4.4 Sheet 36B	1916 September 1		Church Services for men not of the line	
	2		Parades under O.C. Coy. Training for Coy's away on reserve	
	3		Inspection of Small Arms Ammunition by O/C Coy. R.E.O. inspection of equipment	
	4		B Coy relieved A Coy in AVION SECTOR night of 4/5 a NATOR & HOLT Hosts command of Left Front	
	5		13 O.R.s wounded. Gen. Henry saw shelling of enemy on MERICOURT Ridge (Anti-Camp)	
	6		2/Lieut M.M. GERSON joined Battn from Base. Posted to A Coy	
	8		Leperation of S.B.R. & Fitting & efficiency.	
			2/Lieut C. THOMPSON joined from Base depot. Posted to C Coy.	
	10		C Coy relieved D Coy in MERICOURT SECTOR (ANTI SNIPE) night 10/11	
	13		Gas A Coy & wounded 2 Coy 3 Coy A Coy	
			Protest inspection of "B" Coy & fitting & efficiency	
	14		Lieut H.C. THOMPSON joined from Base. Posted to "B" Coy	
	15		2/Lieut TIMPSON transferred from "C" Coy to "A" Coy	
	16		Lieut N.G. KIRWOOD transferred from B Coy. M.B. E.G.Bks. wound	
			Posted to E Coy.	
	22		"C" Coy in Canada Camp (MERICOURT SECTOR) nights 16/17	
			2/Lt Jn Powell "A" Coy wounded to U.K (sick)	
	25		D. Coy from Reserve relieved A Coy in Right Bde Secto afternoon of 25th night of 25/26th A Coy (commanded by Capt E.G. Forbes) sent in relief	

(Continued)

Army Form C. 2118.

WAR DIARY
or
INTELLIGENCE SUMMARY.
(Erase heading not required.)

SHEET 2.

Place	Date	Hour	Summary of Events and Information	Remarks and references to Appendices
Ref Sheet 44A SW /20000 Barrage baselines T28 & T5 20 T7 28 T5 50 Advanced Enemy Wire T28-35 80 Sunken Flank T17 a 30 50 OBJECTIVE TRIUMPHOYA SCOTIA, BRITANNIA & BRANDY TRENCHES in T24 & 30 W of FRESNOY			The Barrage was to lift ↑ attack Positions in OTTOWA TRENCH and establish forming up these at junction of BRUNSWICK TRENCH & CANADA ALLEY, each platoon communicating between troop & in battery Position, 2 mins before Zero, under 2/Lieut P. Fulton covering between left flank of jumping off front attach as supposed by 7OT & QUEBEC TRENCHES to assist flanks by attack. The enemy anticipating attack to meet this took his own barrage back 4 minute all 12 midnight the pre Zero - preliminary intense bombardment from 64,000 rounds in rear of Objectives. The barrage was then lifted 200 yards on to TORTOISE TRENCH & MY ACHEVILLE and clear of this was maintained for 43 minutes to permit the operation of the cavalry on objective. Heavy shelling by enemy between 39 prisoners being taken and sent to Bde. much material acquired. Heavy losses were caused among the enemy in after.	
	27		N.B. NW of T21 T35 at am the troops were mounted, Raiders & tried hard truce hand nil. enemy communication, and no advance from the enemy was made on S.O.S. signal.	
	26		at 1.20 am on morning of 28th, the enemy attempted a counter attack, but was held by most heavy trench mortar & 3 am and 5.30 am. Enemy first enemy positions attempted by light & steady at 7.30 am. The advance companies relieved by 28th Battn Canadian at Bolta Hd. The relief was completed by W. By 12 noon when units in the relieving Battalion where in the water they assumed responsibility. 120,000 rds S.A.A. expected during operator	
SCOTTS CAMP CARENCY X 16 d 90.10				

(continued)

Army Form C. 2118.

WAR DIARY
or
INTELLIGENCE SUMMARY.
(Erase heading not required.)

SHEET 3

Place	Date	Hour	Summary of Events and Information	Remarks and references to Appendices
	29		During the month no fresh MG. work was carried out to N.S. of U.6.8. and no consolidation important. The Coy H.Q. Posts N.8. 8.29 w.7.5. Stables are also being built as also the sleeping dug outs used by men now on not according to programme.	

All Crookston
Captain & Adjutant
20th Bn M.G.C.

20TH BATTALION.
MACHINE GUN
CORPS.
Date 29.9.18.

WAR DIARY
or
INTELLIGENCE SUMMARY
(Erase heading not required.)

Army Form C. 2118.

20th BATTALION MACHINE GUN

20th Batt. Winnipeg Can. Exp. Force

Place	Date 1916 October	Hour	Summary of Events and Information	Remarks and references to Appendices
SCOTTS CAMP CAIRENCY (Rays 61 and B) X.16.a.4.2.	1/2		3 Companies billeting two in Rever Marquant & Achwile section	
	3.	730	In accordance with arrangement previously made in concurrence between Officers Comdg near units & the Enemy Battalion, "B" "C" "D" Companies moved forward and occupied positions formerly occupied to assume Infantry roles. Advanced Battn H.Q. was established at H.Q. 9th Batt. in Left front ("B" Coy) at S.16.a.10.9. at 1930. A "C" moved to Left Reserve at SCOTTS CAMP H.Q. moved & Advanced Batt H.Q. in instructions. This Company awaiting orders for action as & when required.	
(SHOWOAT)			GIVENCHY.	
	5		Advance Batt H.Q. returned to SCOTTS CAMP, arriving at 0315.	
	6		"C" Coy in Arctic Cellars and to be known as GIVENCHY was relieved by Companies of the 13th Bm M.G.C. leaving the section.	
	7		"B" Coy left front relieved and "D" Coy Right centre relieved under orders to reach rest billeting	
Right 4B.	7		Battalion moved to/a THIEULOYE on relief. Transport leaving Battalion marching with Transport.	
	8		Reorganising and making up gaps. En route. of nooperation.	
	9/10		Training	
	10		Major No ENURON from Base before proceeding to ENGLAND for 6 months leave of G.S.	
	14		Lieut. POTTER & Lieut. W. FORBES	

WAR DIARY

INTELLIGENCE SUMMARY
(Erase heading not required.)

Army Form C. 2118.
20th BATTALION MACHINE GUN CORPS

Place	Date	Hour	Summary of Events and Information	Remarks and references to Appendices
At THEUVRE	14		Major W.L. OWEN joined Battalion from 57th Battalion and took over command of H.Q.	
	14/19		Training, chiefly tactical schemes during morning and musketry training in every afternoon.	
	20.		Church Service for all.	
	21/26		Training continued.	
	27/30		Church Service. Training continued.	
	28/30		Battalion moved to CAMBRAI and came under the command of 9 C.C.	
	31		Third Army and XVII Corps.	

Audrey M.
Captain & Adjutant
20th Bn M.G.C.

WAR DIARY
or
INTELLIGENCE SUMMARY.
(Erase heading not required.)

Army Form C. 2118.

20 Bn M. G. Corps

Vol 9

Place	Date November 1918	Hour	Summary of Events and Information	Remarks and references to Appendices
CAMBRAI (AWOINGT)	1/2		Battalion in rest Billets. Party of instructors known to Havrincourt area.	
	3		Battalion with transport moved by road to RIEUX	
RIEUX	4		" " " at SOMMAING	
SOMMAING	7		" " " " MARESCHES	
MARESCHES	8		" " " " ST WAAST	
ST WAAST	9		" " " " FERNIES	
FERNIES	10		Returned HQ moved to LA GROSELLE. "A" & "D" Coys to Bn offrs Supply at MAUBERTON FARM at K.10. (Ref Sheet 51/M0000) "C" Coy to Rgtl. Sy. Htrs at K.21.b.30.70. The guns of "A" & "D" companies were helped to the bne. along the forms belts. Owing to the system of they were not brought effectively with the enemy. Fire plans and schemes attempted to come as effectively on the left of Bn were fired on enemy in BETTIGNIES and ground between Mon MAUBERGE rd and K.9.a. Guns on B "D" Coy K.9.d. Guns in neighbourhood of FORT de LEVEQUE and K.15 & K.10.	
	11		At 11.00 a.m. Troops fire ceased on the Bttn. front. Enemy dispositions on all their front received & Bttn. notes further orders. Front dispositions to Front line.	
	12		Troops fire ceased at 11.00. Troops take over on the...	

Army Form C. 2118.

WAR DIARY
INTELLIGENCE SUMMARY.

(Erase heading not required.)

Instructions regarding War Diaries and Intelligence Summaries are contained in F. S. Regs., Part II. and the Staff Manual respectively. Title pages will be prepared in manuscript.

Place	Date	Hour	Summary of Events and Information	Remarks and references to Appendices
	13		At here 13th of FEIGNIES after the day in FEIGNIES up, [illeg.] awaiting the general fatigues.	
			Arrangements made to clean, burnt myself was found during the morning and reconnoitred & changing in the afternoon.	
	14		Companies billets were unknown, bright work, inspected & FEIGNIES.	
	15		Reconnaissance Training. Company in own training all guns unpacked etc.	
	16		Working and reconnaissance Training.	
			Changing during morning and Reconnaissance Training.	
	17		Reconnaissance Training. 13th & 14th & 15th 6.7 Bn. inspected by 6. Bde. [illeg.]	
	19/22		from the Divisional School 2/25 Th. Bn. during 19th N.B. FEIGNIES 2/25	
			at 11.00 a.m. BRAY & TILLUL on LA PISSOTIAU	
	23		Battalion marched from FEIGNIES	
			(of mt. VILLCIENNES 1/100TH	
LA PISSOTIAU	24		Battalion marched from PISSOTIAU at 9.30 and ST VAAST WARGNIES-LE-GRAND - VILLERS	
			Battalion marched from PISSOTIAU & SEPMERIES	
			POL - MARECHES & SEPMERIES.	
SEPMERIES	25		Battalion marched at 9.00 on YSNOEGIES - SAU&ZOIR - MONTRÉCOURT - ST AUBERT & BIEVROU AVESNES.	
	26		Battalion arrived at AVESNES forming from this station	
AVESNES-LES-AUBERT	27		Battalion marched from AVESNES at 9.00 via RIEUX-HAMIE & BEAVIS on RONAL BARRACKS at CAMBRAI	
CAMBRAI	28		Battalion remained at CAMBRAI	
	29		Battalion preceded by road Paris declaring area at MARICUX	

WAR DIARY
or
INTELLIGENCE SUMMARY.

Army Form C. 2118.

Place	Date	Hour	Summary of Events and Information	Remarks and references to Appendices
GHQ ARMY	29		[illegible handwritten entries] Major T.G. Owen M.C. Capt R.O. Mc. LEAMON	
	30			

WAR DIARY

INTELLIGENCE SUMMARY.

(Erase heading not required.)

Place	Date	Hour	Summary of Events and Information	Remarks and references to Appendices
MARIEUX	1918			
	Jul 1		Major HQ Brown assumed Command of Bn in place of Lt Col J.C. Wrath who proceeded on leave	
	3		to Command A.B. Coy. Lieut E.O. Morgan joined Battn and posted to 'C' Coy	
	4		Organization of Salvage parties	
	7		Received an honour roll Committee at Hqrs of 10 offrs to keep roll to	
	8		Date	
	13		Lecture - "Artillery" by Lt Col C. B. Zermatt	
	14		Church Services	
	15		2/Lt C.E.W. Johnson transferred + posted to 'D' Coy	
	16		2/Lt W. McLelan + 2/Lt A.S. Wright joined + posted to 'A.B.' Coys respectively	
	22		Church Service. 10 OR went on leave	
	23		Lecture on recent Work in France by Major Z 199-194 + 2 Lieut C.E. Lewis	
			2 OR reinforcements	
			Church Services	
			10 OR reinforcements	
			Church Service. Cinematographic	
			Church Services	

A.W. Brown Major
Comdg 20th Bn M.G.C.

D 148/23   17

H.Q.
20th Division

I forward herewith my War Diary for January, 1918.

G. Hayes
Lieut Col
1/2/1918   Comdg 11th D.L.I.

WAR DIARY
INTELLIGENCE SUMMARY.
(Erase heading not required.)

Army Form C. 2118.

20th BATTALION MACHINE GUN COY

Place	Date	Hour	Summary of Events and Information	Remarks and references to Appendices
MARIEUX	Jan 1919			
	1		Veterinary horses inspected all unsound in the Battalion to be cast for demobilization	
	5		Church Service	
	12		Church Service	
	13		36 men proceeded to UK for demobilization	
	15		Church Service	
	18		36 men proceeded to UK for demobilization	
	20		"	
	25		G.O.C. 20th Division inspected Battalion	
	25		1 Officer + 46 O.R's proceeded to UK for demobilization	
	26		Church Service	
	28		1 Officer + 23 O.R's proceeded to UK for demobilization	
			30 Horses Class "Y" sent to DIEPPE for demobilization	
	29		During the present party the month French Return in the neighbourhood of MARIEUX, an average of 60 men daily Employed on training &c carried on away to billets of the month. The following classes being held: Skating, French, Book-Keeping, Building Elementary, French Advanced, Lectures, Vocational, Physical Training	

WM Campbell / Lieut Colonel

20th Batt. Machine Gun Corps.   No. M.G.5/605.

SECRET

20th Division "A"

      Herewith copy of War Diary for February 1919.

                                                Captain & Adjutant.
1-3-19.   for Lt.Col.Commanding 20th Batt.M.G.Corps.

WAR DIARY
or
INTELLIGENCE SUMMARY.

Army Form C. 2118.

20 Bn M.G. Corps

Place	Date	Hour	Summary of Events and Information	Remarks and references to Appendices
MARIEUX Zoes II Shed 23	Feb 1/9		Church Service.	
	2		NCO proceeds to UK for demobilization	
	6		HQ Coy returned to Bn for demobilization	
	8		Church Service	
	9		1 Officer + 13 ORs proceeded to UK for demobilization	
	15		Church Service	
	17		1 Officer + 19 ORs proceeded to UK for demobilization	
	21		2 Officers + 4 ORs " " "	
	22		Church Service	
	28		1 Officer + 15 ORs proceeded to UK for demobilization	

Captain & Adjutant
20th Bn. M.G.C.

www.ingramcontent.com/pod-product-compliance
Lightning Source LLC
Chambersburg PA
CBHW081245170426
43191CB00034B/2044